DEEP ROOTS?

A fresh look at the origins of some Quaker ideas

by

Simon Webb

First published in 2007
by Simon Webb

To Durham Friends

ISBN 978-0-9544759-2-5

Also by Simon Webb:

Open House: A Quaker tale in verse
ISBN 978-0-9544759-0-1
Price £3

George Fox in Barbados
ISBN 978-0-9544759-1-8
Price £2

Published by Simon Webb:

The Captivity of Elizabeth Hanson:
A Quaker Kidnapped by
Native Americans in 1725
by Samuel Bownas
ISBN 978-0954475932
Price £5

Available from:
The Quaker Bookshop
Friends House
173-177 Euston Road
London NW1 2BJ

INTRODUCTION

Given the tradition of outward mildness that has accompanied the Quakers through much of their history, it is easy to forget how radical the ideas of the first Quakers were. In seventeenth century England, when church and state were trying to dictate every detail of exactly how the British should come to terms with their God, George Fox preached about the power of an individual's own direct experience of the divine. In an early modern world where people routinely deferred to any man in holy orders, Fox and his followers interrupted clergymen during their sermons and suggested, in effect, that the class of specially trained and salaried priests should be abolished. In place of 'ordained' ministers, the early Quakers wanted to see everyone ministering spontaneously, according to the promptings of the Inner Light.

The Quaker ideas of the Inner Light and the priesthood of all believers can be identified as forms of *mysticism*, and of *anti-clericalism*. Their radical nature was seen by the authorities in Britain and elsewhere as a threat, and led to long years of persecution for Quakers.

But are these ideas original and, if not, where did they come from? What was the route whereby George Fox in particular acquired them? In short, what were George Fox's influences? Fox often seems to be acting and thinking in an entirely new and independent way. Was this really the case?

Reading George Fox's *Journal*, one gets a sense of a man ruled by deep spiritual insights: what one does not get is the sense of a man who has been greatly influenced by much extensive reading outside of the scriptures. Fox's seeming lack of reliance on theological reading contrasts strongly with what we know of many other people in Western European history who, like Fox, could be called religious revolutionaries. John Wycliffe, the inspiration for the Lollards, was a highly-qualified academic as well as an ordained priest. Martin Luther, the father of the Reformation, was a German monk, a scholar capable of translating the scriptures into his own language, and an academic teacher, extremely well-read in religion. The seed of the Methodist movement, in some ways comparable to

1

Quakerism, can be said to have been sown among the dreaming spires of Oxford University, which John Wesley himself attended: at Christ Church College, Wesley and his 'Holy Club' of fellow-students prayed hard and methodically, but also read widely, and not just in the Christian classics.

With Wycliffe, Luther and Wesley, as well as many other religious luminaries of the past, we are able to point to a set of authors, writings and ideas about which they must have known, because of the education we know that they had. This is not really the case with George Fox. Compared to Wycliffe, Luther and Wesley, George Fox had a very restricted education. He even seems to have harboured a suspicion of education and of educated people, particularly men of the cloth: early in his *Journal*, he asserts that 'being bred at Oxford or Cambridge [is] not enough to fit or qualify men to be ministers of Christ'.

Looking back on the 1640s, he tells us how:

I was to bring people off from Jewish ceremonies, and from heathenish fables, and from men's inventions and worldly doctrines, by which they blew the people about this way and the other, from sect to sect; and from all their beggarly rudiments, with their schools and colleges for making ministers of Christ,-who are indeed ministers of their own making, but not of Christ's...

(all quotations from Fox's *Journal* are from the Rufus M. Jones 1908 edition, available online in the Christian Classics Ethereal Library: http://www.ccel.org)

Fox was undoubtedly an 'original' (as William Penn stated) and a largely self-taught man, but it is still possible to trace the way in which he was influenced by earlier Christian thinkers, whose ideas had been passed down to his generation through the medium of the book. The main threads in George Fox's thinking that are traced in *this* book are his mysticism, and what I have called his anti-clericalism.

MYSTICISM

Mysticism seems to be a very ancient element in human experience. Broadly speaking, it is to do with the moments when human beings break out of the comparative greyness of everyday life and enter into the profound light and dark, and the intense colour, of the divine world. In monotheistic religions like Christianity, mystical experiences tend to involve some sort of contact with God, or with God's agents the angels or the saints. There is also a long tradition of mystics seeing symbolic creatures and personages, and objects and places filled with tremendous significance.

In the Old Testament, experiences of direct contact with the divine are usually referred to not as examples of mysticism, but of prophecy. Prophecy in this context has a much wider meaning than that which is now commonly understood. Biblical prophets were not just concerned with prophesying the future, like the stock-market prophets and political pundits of today. The Old Testament prophets told their truth about the past, the present *and* the future, a truth inspired by what they learned as a result of their special contact with Yahweh, the God of Israel.

The Old Testament prophets claimed personal authority by virtue of their mystical visions, and were sometimes allowed to act as human bridges between the divine and the political spheres. In the books of Samuel, the eponymous prophet chooses David as the future king of Israel, thus reasserting his God's right to make the selection. This is seen by Saul, the reigning king, as a threat to his authority. Samuel's support legitimates David's deployment of what might today be called guerilla tactics. Samuel proves himself to be one of the three most powerful men of Israel, yet the source of his power can be traced back to his receipt of God's direct word from childhood.

Later in the Old Testament, Ezekiel and Daniel have notable visions, some of a very strange nature, which are understood to have both religious and political relevance. Daniel not only pacifies lions and interprets other people's dreams – he also has his own personal vision, which takes place after a long and painful period of fasting. Ezekiel is consulted by the leaders of the exiled Israelites, and through his visions he gives them reasons for their

3

captivity, instructions on how to conduct themselves in the present, and cause for hope in the future.

Despite the fact of their vital role within the nation of Israel, Old Testament prophets often seem rather isolated – they are men apart, living according to different rules, separated off because of their special gift, or curse.

With the New Testament, and the coming of Jesus, the element of direct communication with God reappears in the Bible, but in a new way: Jesus is not so much a prophet, as the image of God himself to many Christians. This gives his prophetic statements a unique authority: he is not communicating with God – he *is* God.

Other New Testament figures who have mystical experiences do not seem to be as isolated as some of the prophets of the Old Testament: it is as if the first Christians have entered a new world where visions and miracles are more a part of everyday life. The visions of Peter and Paul all seem to point in the same direction – they support the idea of Jesus, emphasise the significance of his life and explain the details of his message. An example of a highly practical and informative vision occurs in the Book of Acts, where Peter sees:

...a certain vessel descending upon him, as it had been a great sheet knit at the four corners, and let down to the earth: wherein were all manner of fourfooted beasts of the earth, and wild beasts, and creeping things, and fowls of the air.

And there came a voice to him, Rise, Peter; kill, and eat.

(Acts 10:11-13. All Biblical quotations are from the King James Version)

This vision, which comes to a hungry and sleeping apostle, is a timely answer to the vexed question of what Jews who had become Christians should be allowed to eat. Peter is at first shocked by the message of his dream – he has always kept kosher up to this point. We are to understand that the vision overrides the dietary strictures of Leviticus, as well as centuries of Jewish tradition. This is a function that visionary messages often perform – they offer a new and surprising direction to the visionary who experiences them.

4

A more famous early example of a mystical vision is Saint Paul's experience on the road to Damascus. Here, Paul sees and hears Jesus, although those accompanying him do not. The experience causes him to fall down and to become temporarily blind. The event is strange, unexpected and, as far as we know, unprecedented in Paul's experience. It changes him completely: he now becomes the opposite of the persecutor of the new Christian sect that he was when he set out. The double-edged nature of his new visionary gift is very evident – he now sees better spiritually, yet he has become temporarily blind to the familiar sights of the everyday world. He has been given an extraordinary power, yet he is also helpless and has to be nursed by some of the very people he had originally set out to hurt.

In his second letter to the Corinthians, Paul hints at further mystical experiences, where he is 'caught up to the third heaven'. He refuses, however, to gloat about these new visions that have been vouchsafed to him, and emphasizes the pain that comes along with the spiritual gain: 'lest I should be exalted above measure through the abundance of the revelations, there was given to me a thorn in the flesh, the messenger of Satan to buffet me' (II Cor. 12:7).

Although George Fox is very similar to Saint Paul in many respects, Fox's mystical conversion experience is very different from Paul's. There is no suggestion that Paul was unhappy with his earlier task of rooting out Christians, and it is clear that his conversion cut him off from a promising career, perhaps at the Temple in Jerusalem.

By contrast, George Fox is in his own personal wilderness, and at his wit's end when he is first given his 'Openings'. He seems to be suffering from a profound form of what we would now call depression. Fox's is not a sudden all-in-one experience, like Paul's on the road to Damascus: Fox descends slowly into the dark well of his own mental condition and, having reached the bottom, becomes strong enough to scoop up a generous helping of the water of truth.

The type of mysticism that was most relevant to George Fox and the early Quakers is to do with the direct experience of the divine given to such individuals as St Paul, and Fox himself. For Paul and George, their mystical experiences and insights were aspects of lives spent in service to the Gospel.

There is, however, another, rather less direct form of Christian mysticism: this is the speculative, elaborated, literary mysticism described by authors and teachers who examine mystical ideas and their ramifications in depth. The authors of works of this type may not have mystical experiences of the Damascus variety: mystical insights can also be gained through contemplation, imagination and study.

Among European mystics whose thoughts have been passed down to us in written form, the German Meister Eckhart is one of the most attractive. In a series of sermons and tractates, he sets out his conceptions of God, the soul and the Kingdom in remarkably accessible terms. Also in the fourteenth century, the anonymous British author of *The cloud of unknowing* examined the rewards and the pitfalls of the believer's mystical journey to God in extraordinary detail, and with great sensitivity.

Like George Fox's contemporary, the philosopher Baruch Spinoza, Eckhart was accused of heresy, and can be seen as a kind of pantheist, detecting the presence of God in every aspect of the physical world. Part of the attractiveness for modern readers of both Eckhart's works, and *The cloud of unknowing* is that they both seem to occupy a world of thought and feeling that goes beyond Christianity. Both Eckhart and the author of *The cloud*, for instance, entertain notions about nothingness and negation of the self, that must strike a chord with any Buddhist readers.

There are many inter-faith parallels in the mystical sphere: Descartes' and Spinoza's ideas were inspired by geometry, and Jacob Boehme and the English Behmenist Jane Lead produced diagrams to illustrate some of their insights. The Jewish Kabbalists also used diagrams, and Buddhist mandalas can be seen as geometrical representations of religious conceptions. It is also possible to unravel the mystical worlds of William Blake's longer poems into charts of correspondences.

St Paul seems to have resisted the temptation to elaborate his Damascene vision into a diagram or a Kabbalistic system. He often referred to his experience on the road to Damascus, but he set out its significance in a direct, persuasive way. He made use of his conversion experience as Christian propaganda in the best sense: he wanted everyone to share the meaning of what he had seen and heard, and he refrained from wrapping it up in esoteric references.

Jacob Boehme

Jacob Boehme, who died in the same year George Fox was born, built a vast body of writings on the elaboration of his mystical experiences. He is also a mystic whose writings have often been cited as a possible inspiration for George Fox and the early Quakers.

Sometime in the year 1600, Boehme somehow became hypnotized by the reflection of the sunlight in a pewter dish. The effect of this mundane sight on his mind was profound and life-changing. It seemed to open up some sort of map of the universe to this humble German cobbler, who went on to write voluminous works about what he had seen.

It is tempting to put Jacob Boehme's vision down to some form of migraine. Migraine sufferers sometimes experience hallucinations, and the effect of a sudden bright light on the eyes of a sufferer in the throes of a migraine attack can be quite spectacular. The visions of the twelfth-century mystic Hildegard of Bingen have also been attributed to migraine. A less kindly observer might attribute visions such as Boehme's to mental illness.

If some sort of health problem was the origin of Jacob Boehme's visions, it hardly matters. What matters is that he elaborated what he saw, or thought he saw, into a unique and labyrinthine view of God's universe.

The evidence that George Fox was familiar with the works of Jacob Boehme is slender. Lodowick Muggleton, a contemporary of George Fox and a leading light of the

Muggletonian religious sect, asserted that the Quakers he knew were reading Boehme. Rufus M. Jones points this out in the notes to his edition of George Fox's *Journal*. Muggleton's *A looking-glass for George Fox* (1667), part of an acrimonious exchange of pamphlets between Fox and Muggleton, includes the latter's statement that 'Jacob Behmont's Books were the chief books that the Quakers bought, for there is the Principle or Foundation of their Religion'. In the context of seventeenth century England, Muggleton's assertion can be read as a calculated insult. At that time the Quakers, like most Christian groups throughout history, were busy claiming direct spiritual descent from the oldest possible Christian ancestry – Jesus and the Apostles. Meanwhile, Muggleton tries to give them a rather upstart character by claiming that the recently translated works of a cobbler are the 'Principle or Foundation of their Religion'.

Rufus M. Jones was an expert in the field of mysticism, which he rightly saw as a unifying factor among the religions of the world. The *Looking glass* pamphlet is one of Jones's most important sources for a link between Boehme and Fox, but unfortunately this document is by its nature unreliable, and very much bound to the context of the pamphlet war then current. Muggleton's words are bitter and combative, and, in the section where he mentions Jacob Boehme, rather petty. He complains that the Quakers refuse to buy and read his (Muggleton's) books, 'though they cost ever so much pains the writing, and cost the printing'. He also argues that his own followers are reluctant to lend their books to Quakers because they might 'abuse' them 'very basely' by 'writing upon the Margent'. Muggleton cites the case of one Thomas Barnes, who lent a book to the Quaker Thomas Taylor, only to find that it had been defaced in this way.

Muggleton cites a letter from the Quaker William Smith as his source for the story that the Quakers bought 'Behmont's' books 'for they cannot go beyond that, but there they build'; he goes on to imply that his correspondent William Smith is far beyond George Fox in his knowledge of 'Behmont'.

As for other books Muggleton says that the Quakers have bought, he claims there are 'none of any value'. The author of *The looking glass* also complains that the Quakers know no 'Heavenly Secrets', such as 'what the true God is in his Form and Nature...what the Right Devil is...the place of Hell...the Residence of Heaven...'. Such 'Heavenly Secrets' are, according to Muggleton, to be found in his own works. These 'secrets' are also very like the mystical preoccupations of Jacob Boehme.

If the Quakers could only have opened their minds to Muggleton and bought just one of his books, the author claims, they would have made it their:

Church-Bible, and taken [their] text out of it every time [they] meet, [their] Hearers would have edified more by [their] reading a Chapter in that when [they] meet together, than by all the Speakings that ever they have heard in their lives, it would have cost [them] but ten shillings, [they] might have had it out of the Church Stock...then [their] light within; and [their] Christ within [them], would have come to nothing, and so [they] would cheat the people no longer...'

Apart from Lodowick Muggleton, the other evidence for a Boehme-Fox link that Rufus Jones points to is a passage that seems to betray Fox's knowledge of Boehme's book, *De rerum natura (The Universal Signature)*. In the relevant passage, Fox recounts a deep mystical experience that brings him close to knowing 'the hidden unity in the Eternal Being':

I was at a stand in my mind whether I should practise physic for the good of mankind, seeing the nature and virtues of things were so opened to me by the Lord.

A similar passage in the first chapter of Boehme's *Universal Signature* promises knowledge of the 'essence of all essences':

...man...may not only learn to know himself, but therein also he may learn to know the essence of all essences; for by the external form of all creatures, by their instigation, inclination, and desire, also by their sound, voice, and speech which they utter, the hidden spirit is known...

(Jacob Boehme, *The Universal Signature*, translated by William Law)

9

The key to both these passages, in Fox and in Boehme, is the so-called 'doctrine of signatures'. Boehme's writings tend to complicate this idea, but in essence it is very simple. The doctrine states that, when he created the world, God left clues as to the identity of its creator scattered about his creation, much as an artist might half-hide his signature somewhere in a painting. It is the job of the faithful Christian to recognize these signatures for what they are. The signatures, once identified, reinforce faith and also confer other benefits on mankind.

The commonest use of the signatures doctrine in seventeenth century Europe related to medicine: herbalists were supposed to be able to 'read' the virtues of a plant in the natural shape of the plant itself. God was supposed to have fashioned the plant into a useful message: this proved that God was talking to humanity through nature, offering them his help.

A good example of how this doctrine was applied to medicine is found in the traditional use of the various species of liverworts or Hepatica. These have leaves with three lobes, like the human liver, and were once used to treat liver complaints (liverwort extracts are now known to be toxic in high doses).

The doctrine of signatures was indeed central to Boehme's ideas, and George Fox seems to have been familiar with it, but the doctrine could easily have come to Fox by some other route than via the writings of the Silesian mystic. These pseudo-scientific ideas were pretty commonplace in Europe until modern times.

Francis Daniel Pastorius, the seventeenth-century Quaker hero of Whittier's poem *The Pennsylvania pilgrim*, calls to mind the doctrine of signatures when he walks in his garden:

> For, by the lore of Gorlitz' gentle sage,
> With the mild mystics of the dreamy age
> He read the herbal signs of nature's page

The similarity between Fox's vision of a 'hidden unity' and the passage Jones cites from *De rerum natura* can also be put down to the nature of such visions which, according to William James, are often very similar even when experienced by adherents of other faiths. James, who was very widely read in the subject, compares accounts of many profound mystical experiences in his *Varieties of religious experience* (Lectures XVI and XVII). Drawing on the literatures of mysticism in many cultures, James discovers fascinating examples of states where individuals feel a unity with, and knowledge of, God and the universe that cannot be attained in the realm of cool, rational thought. James quotes from Charles Kingsley:

When I walk the fields, I am oppressed now and then with an innate feeling that everything I see has a meaning, if I could but understand it. And this feeling of being surrounded by truths which I cannot grasp amounts to indescribable awe sometimes...

In his account of his experience with the hallucinogenic drug mescaline, Aldous Huxley has a similar vision of the completeness and inclusiveness of the universe, in his case caused by the hypnotic effect on his drugged consciousness of the sight of a vase of flowers.

I.M. Lewis, in his book on ecstatic religion, quotes from the experience of an 'Eskimo' shaman whose first sense of his special power is remarkably similar to both Boehme's and Fox's visions:

I could see and hear in a totally different way. I had gained my enlightenment, the shaman's light of brain and body.

Compare this to Fox's famous statement:

All things were new; and all the creation gave unto me another smell than before, beyond what words can utter.

Like Fox, the Arctic mystic had undergone a period of physical and mental suffering before his enlightenment occurred.

Eugene d'Aquili identifies the tendency of people in a mystical state to see a unity in creation as a 'cognitive operator'. In this case the relevant 'cognitive operator' is what he calls the 'holistic operator'. This, together with the 'causal operator' operates to give the mystic a feeling of the unity of creation under God's control.

Jacob Boehme was a mystic like George Fox, and as such he received many of his insights into the nature of the universe from visions. But their attempts to give accounts of their visions show up the most profound differences between the two men: Boehme's reports are by no means as straightforward as George Fox's tales of his 'Openings'. Whereas Fox was often lost for words with which to describe his most profound visions, Boehme insisted on unravelling his into very extensive writings. For Boehme the universe swarmed with numbers, symbols, secrets, magical words and alchemical compounds.

As well as the doctrine of signatures, Boehme has his own version of the ancient idea of the four elements, of which all things were supposed to have been made. Whereas modern scientists believe that things are ultimately made up of atoms and fields, earlier philosophers and physicians thought that all things were made up of fire, air, earth and water. This idea, which can be traced right back to the ancient Greek physician Hippocrates (born circa 450 B.C.) was gloriously revived in the sixteenth and seventeenth centuries, where it inspired, among others, William Shakespeare, the poet and playwright Ben Jonson, and the philosopher Robert Burton, author of *An Anatomy of Melancholy.*

The four elements of fire, air, earth and water were supposed to have their equivalents in four humours or fluids observed to exist in the human body. Air was represented by blood, earth by black bile or melancholy, fire by yellow bile and water by phlegm. Illness and defects of personality were supposed to be caused by an imbalance of the humours. In particular, the illness we now call depression was supposed to be caused by an excess of the melancholy humour.

These ideas might seem bizarre to modern readers, but they were part of Hippocrates' holistic view of the body, and led him to look to poor diet as a possible cause of illnesses. This holistic emphasis, and the idea of preventing illness by a pre-emptive attack on the patient's diet, are in line with modern medical practice. The idea of an imbalance of bodily fluids causing mental illness is remarkably similar to the less speculative modern understanding of, for instance, depression, now thought to be associated in some cases with levels of certain chemicals in the brain.

The idea of the body's four humours was once so widely accepted that traces of it have survived in the English language. We still talk about *temperament* (literally the mixture or *temper* of the humours), about *sanguine* or *phlegmatic* personalities, and about *melancholy* feelings. Into this popular conception of the make-up of mind and body, Jacob Boehme introduced his own ideas about light and darkness, and he also gave the element of fire an especially complex role: for him fire was the giver of both light and heat, and a symbol of anger and desire, among other things.

According to Boehme, Adam, before the creation of Eve, enjoyed a balance of his bodily humours that went beyond mere health and contentment: his mind and body were the perfect receptacles for his soul. With the Fall, the perfectly blended humours of Adam became unbalanced and began to show their individual characteristics, both good and bad. For Boehme, Adam before the fall was an androgynous creature with no teeth, genitals or digestive organs. Eve was created out of him and, in her nature, reflected those aspects of Adam that were forced to detach themselves from him, since he was now no longer perfectly balanced. After the Fall, the light that was once an integral part of man and his world became something elusive, something that must be sought.

Boehme's constant use of the idea of the light is surely one reason why he is often named as a precursor of Quakerism. His idea of the divine light is, however, very different from George Fox's. Boehme seems to see light as a symbol of wisdom, and associates light with Sophia, a female personification of wisdom. Boehme's introduction of Sophia, who sounds something like a pagan goddess, into a complex of ideas including the Creation, the Fall, Jesus and the trinity would seem to be quite alien to George Fox's thought.

For Fox, the Inner Light was something akin to the Holy Spirit, something that brought salvation and comfort. For the early Quakers, wisdom, or at least wisdom as a result of knowledge and learning, was not as central to the gifts of the spirit as was love. In earlier times Sophia was an important aspect of Gnostic teaching, which, among other things, tended to stress knowledge (*gnosis*) as a key to salvation. In this context, *gnosis* sounds similar to Muggleton's 'heavenly secrets'. This is also quite alien to early Quaker ideas. Fox had no interest in promoting elusive Gnostic 'truths': he was concerned to spread the familiar message of the Gospel, which by its nature was accessible to all.

When Christian mysticism reaches the giddy altitude of Boehme's writings, matters such as church services, church buildings, the Reformation and the priesthood appear as if seen from far above, distorted into unfamiliar shapes by a white mist. In particular, the scriptures seem less important than what can be read between their lines, and Jesus seems to be stripped of his human presence and turned into a light, a Holy Grail, an ideal, a breath, or part of some alchemical recipe. Boehme's ideas seem to be so detached from any identifiable social, historical or geographical context that they begin to partake of the atmosphere of modern speculations about superstrings, artificial intelligence and relativity.

For mystics of Boehme's type, conventional language often becomes quite inadequate for the task of describing or explaining what the visionary seeks to express. Boehme developed his own special words for use in his writings, and stretched and twisted the meanings of more familiar words so that, as in the case of Spinoza, the reader feels he may be entering a strange new universe as he tries to keep a grip on meaning.

Jane Lead

Boehme was popular among the English in the seventeenth century, and his posthumous celebrity gave rise to a group called the English Behmenists. (Boehme is also called Behmen: there are in fact many different versions of his surname).

An important English Behmenist was the Norfolk mystic Jane Lead, born in the same year as George Fox. Like Fox, she had an experience of contact with the divine in her teenage years: during a Christmas Eve dance, she heard a voice that told her, 'Cease from this, I have another dance to lead thee in, for this is vanity'. Thus far, her story could almost be the story of a Quaker's convincement – a young girl from a respectable family is called by God to abandon frivolous delights and to pursue some sort of holy mission – 'another dance'.

Lead did not become unusually active in the religious sphere until 1670, the year of her husband's death, when she received the first of three visions of 'the Virgin-Wisdom'. In her third and last vision of this archetypal personage, the Virgin-Wisdom told her, 'I shall now cease to appear in a visible figure unto thee but will not fail to transfigure myself in thy mind and therefore open the Spring of Wisdom and Understanding'. This inner fount was supposed to be the source of Jane Lead's many writings.

In her 1695 book *The Wonders of God's Creation Manifested in the Variety of Eight Worlds,* Jane Lead sets out her sense of the structure of the entire universe, including the eight worlds supposed to be inhabited by the living and the dead. Some of these worlds, the 'Astral or Aerial World', the 'Waterish Elementary World' and the 'Fiery Dark World' remind us of Boehme's fondness for the idea of the four elements and the bodily humours. Likewise, her vision of the Virgin-Wisdom is very like Boehme's Sophia.

Lead's *Wonders* book provides, in part, a detailed account of the fates of various types of saints and sinners after death. Although hers is supposed to be a new and divinely inspired account, she still seems to rely heavily on traditional notions about 'the Elementary Worlds, with their Peculiar Furniture or Inhabitants severally allotted to them'.

Lead's affection for the idea of wisdom, and her assertion that the wisdom that possessed her provided the key to long-hidden truths, shows how far a contemporary English Behmenist could diverge from Quakerism, at least Quakerism as represented in the writings of George Fox.

Fox's Seed or Inner Light, his equivalent to the Virgin-Wisdom of Jane Lead, is surely understood to be located in the human heart from birth, or even before. It may be obscured or forced down by pride, error, or some other factor, but it is not supposed to be absent at any time. Although Fox clearly felt that he had a new message for humanity, he also seems to imply that this is also the same old message that can be found in the scriptures.

In her *Wonders of God's Creation*, Lead asserts that her revelation is a sort of new New Testament, 'given from him, who Was, and Is, and Will be the true Inspirer, to open new Volumes of his Mind, which are not to be less reputed and credited than the foregoing Scriptures'. It is perhaps not surprising that the author of the introduction to this work warns his readers that, 'What is contained in this Treatise...will appear more than ordinarily Strange, to the greatest part of those who shall look upon it'.

One passage from Lead's *Enochian walks* (1694) has a sensuousness, symbolism, and use of allegory that call to mind the medieval dream-poem *The romance of the rose*. She describes her inspiration as a flower:

This is the Plant that hath put forth itself distinct from the outward nature in me. Well known it is by its pleasant scent, qualifying with fragrant love so very sweet and mild that it harmonizes the soul to the degree that it feels no other life than a spiritual Deity. That is the Root which feeds this rosy flower of the mind with a certain kind of balsamic virtue so that its beauty is always of a blushing freshness.

Samuel Butler satirized what may have amounted to a seventeenth-century craze for Behmenism in his poem *Hudibras*. Describing the hero's ludicrous squire, Ralpho, he writes:

> He ANTHROPOSOPHUS, and FLOUD,
> And JACOB BEHMEN understood:
> Knew many an amulet and charm,
> That wou'd do neither good nor harm...

Here 'Anthroposophus' may refer to one Dr. Vaughan, a rector of Bedfordshire, who published his *Anthroposophia Teomagica*, about life after death, in 1650. 'Floud' is almost certainly Robert Fludd (1574-1637) an English astrologer and mystic. Ralpho's belief in amulets and charms is reminiscent of current interest in the supposed healing powers of crystals.

16

Butler mocked Boehme in verse, and the nineteenth-century author Charles Mackay later mocked him in prose, in his *Extraordinary popular delusions and the madness of crowds*. 'Böhmen', as Mackay spells him, appears in his section on 'Alchymists' and is described as having 'buried his brain under the rubbish of metaphysics'. According to Mackay, Böhmen spent his time 'purifying metals one day, and mystifying the Word of God on the next'.

Despite the presence in George Fox's England of such enthusiastic Behmenists as Jane Lead, the conventional nature of some of the Silesian's ideas make a definite link between Fox and Boehme difficult to establish. If, for instance, Fox had shown any interest in the doctrine of the four humours, it could still be argued that he had that interest from some other source - the four humours were a commonplace in the science of the seventeenth century.

There is certainly a stark contrast between the nature of the mysticism promoted by Boehme and his followers, and that experienced by George Fox. Fox's visions seem to have been either of a vast and all-inclusive nature, or, by contrast, very specific and functional. Fox describes his more comprehensive visions in very general terms, almost as if the immensity of his insight was too large to be contained in his memory for very long. His more specific, 'signpost' visions are also very swiftly set out. Boehme and Lead spent a lot more time and effort relating and interpreting their visions through their writings.

The partial testimony of Muggleton, the seventeenth-century English versions of Boehme's works, the contemporary existence of such 'Behmenists' as Jane Lead and the evidence of strikingly similar passages in Boehme and Fox, do not really supply a definitive link between the two men. Rufus Jones, in his *Faith & practice of the Quakers*, describes Boehme's place in the religious landscape against which Fox moved: he then asserts that 'the fundamental ideas of the [Quaker] movement were more or less "in the air" in the Commonwealth period'. It is implied that the ideas of continental mystics such as Boehme were one constituent of the Commonwealth atmosphere.

Braithwaite, paraphrasing Rufus Jones's thoughts on this matter in his *Beginnings of Quakerism*, shows real insight into the nature of George Fox's mind:

...knowledge of Boehme...might readily act on his [Fox's] spirit by way of 'suggestion' and be reproduced in a vivid psychic experience which would be in his mind the sure evidence of its truth.

If Braithwaite's statement is true, it means, of course, that anyone trying to quantify the indebtedness of George Fox's to other thinkers is bound to be baffled – Fox transformed the ideas that came to him into something that is only recognizable as a part of Fox.

It was George Fox's practice to judge what came to him from outside by his own Inner Light. If he found what he saw, heard or read to be worthwhile, he made it his own. In the case of Jacob Boehme, Fox would surely have found many of the Silesian's more outré ideas irrelevant, obscure and even frivolous. If Fox did subject Boehme's ideas to a kind of alchemical refining process in his own mind, this is entirely consistent with the Quaker idea of the Inner Light: the Light not only illuminates the life of the believer – it serves to light his way in life and to help him discern that which speaks to his condition.

ANTI-CLERICALISM

As well as a man of a marked mystical turn of mind, George Fox was a man with revolutionary ideas about the Christian church and how it should be organised. Although the term seems odd when applied to such a compassionate person, George Fox was, strictly speaking, anti-clerical. He wanted to see the end of paid, ordained ministers and their hierarchy that, in England, still reaches up to the very top of government.

The anti-clericalism of Fox and many of his generation was closely allied to the anti-Catholic and anti-Semitic feelings that were unattractive aspects of English Protestantism from the outset. In contemporary writings, both the Roman Catholic Church and the synagogues of the Jews are associated with overly formal, legalistic, corrupt, benighted and hierarchical forms of religion.

English anti-Catholic feeling continued to be rife from the Reformation right up to quite modern times. The *Westminster Confession of Faith*, drawn up as a sort of blueprint for religious reform by some Puritan clergymen in 1646, is quite clear about its attitude to Roman Catholicism:

There is no other head of the Church but the Lord Jesus Christ: nor can the Pope of Rome in any sense be the head thereof; but is that Antichrist, the man of sin and son of perdition...

In 1666 many blamed the Great Fire of London on the Catholics, and in 1681 the words 'but Popish frenzy, which wrought such horrors, is not yet quenched' were added to an inscription on the Monument. This prompted the English Roman Catholic poet Alexander Pope to write:

Where London's column, pointing at the skies,
Like a tall bully, lifts the head and lies
(*Moral Essays*, Epistle iii)

The 'Popish frenzy' inscription was removed in 1831, but anti-Catholic feeling persisted. Even a modern writer like GK Chesterton, who converted to Roman Catholicism in 1922, was compelled to write lucid, scorching critiques of anti-Catholic books and articles. In his essay *The*

Protestant Superstitions he describes a sort of grim parlour-game, in which English Roman Catholic readers amuse themselves by trying to guess:

...at exactly which line of an article...we shall find the Dean of St Paul's introducing the Antidote to Antichrist; or the Popish Plot Revealed..

The first Puritans got their name from their attempts to promulgate a 'pure' form of Protestantism in England: a form purged of many practices that they regarded as Roman Catholic 'excrescences'. It seems that these 'excrescences' included elaborate church decorations and certain kinds of religious art, devotion to the Pope, any overly enthusiastic devotion to the Virgin Mary, the use of the Latin Vulgate Bible, and the enforced celibacy of the priesthood. Some hard-core Puritans also disliked devotion to the saints, and were very disappointed that the Church of England still retained some key features of the Roman Catholic Church, such as bishops and archbishops.

The continuing strength of anti-Catholic feeling in George Fox's time is hardly surprising, given the historical context: the Reformation Church of England was built on Henry VIII's inability to agree with the Pope. The disastrous Civil War that Fox had witnessed at close hand had begun partly because Charles II and William Laud, his Archbishop of Canterbury, were suspected of getting nearer to Rome. Anti-Catholic feeling was bound up with English patriotism at this time, as was anti-Semitism: some viewed both the English Jews and the Catholics as dangerous and unwelcome aliens, almost by definition.

If anti-Catholic feeling is to be counted as one of the roots of early Quakerism, then it is a particularly deep root. Some aspects of Roman Catholicism had found their critics in England even before the country became part of the Reformation, at a time when nearly all of Western Europe was Roman Catholic.

John Wycliffe

Wycliffe has long been regarded as the great-grandfather of the English Reformation or, more flatteringly, as its 'Morning Star'. Some of his more radical ideas were remarkably close to the ideas of early Friends.

Wycliffe lived in the fourteenth century, when the Latin Christianity of Western Europe, dominated by the figure of the Pope, was in a state of crisis. As Barbara Tuchman demonstrates in her book *A distant mirror*, the Europe of the fourteenth century was beset by horrendous crises, including plagues, insurrections, pogroms, exploitation of the peasantry, and wars. It would have been very surprising if the Roman Church had not suffered its own problems during that century.

The church of Wycliffe's time was heir to a noble heritage. Throughout the Dark Ages, the church had helped to preserve the best of the classical civilization of Greece and Rome in Western Europe, while the eastern remnant of the old Roman Empire continued in the form of the Byzantine Empire. The monks and priests of the West had kept literacy and culture alive, and the monarchs who came to dominate Europe often relied on the ecclesiastical class to act as administrators, diplomats, lawyers, archivists, communicators - even propagandists.

The Christian rulers of Europe looked to the church to legitimate their power and to justify their actions with theological arguments, much as King David had looked to the prophet Samuel for divinely-inspired support. In return, the church itself became very rich and powerful, and bishops, archbishops and popes became big-league political players. In the fourteenth century the class of secular, non-aristocratic administrators, politicians and businessmen was beginning to come of age, however, and was developing its own culture, opinions and claims to power.

A perfect example of the secular man of humble origins who achieved status for himself in the England of the time is the poet Geoffrey Chaucer. The son of a wine-merchant, Chaucer rose to become a courtier of sorts: for a time he was also the man in charge of the vital wool exports that were shipped out from the Port of London.

The Prologue to Chaucer's *Canterbury Tales* reveals the misgivings about the church that were current when it was written. Many of the pilgrims to Canterbury described in Chaucer's *Prologue* are professionally connected to the church in some way, and it must be said that most of these are not very encouraging examples of church employees. The Monk is only interested in travelling about and living a high old life with his rich friends. The Prioress is young and pretty, and makes sure everybody knows it. The Nuns' Priest (an essential adjunct to a nunnery since nuns, unlike monks, could not become priests and conduct services among themselves) re-tells a farmyard tale from Aesop that suggests that he at least fancies himself as a cockerel among the hens. Chaucer's Parson is the only really virtuous churchman, and the rewards for his exemplary virtue are provincial obscurity, poverty and isolation.

Chaucer's contemporary poet, William Langland, is merciless in his portrayal of venial priests in the Prologue to his *Piers Plowman*, describing how, in the wake of the plague, some country priests cheat their flocks, then run off to the capital to sing masses for the souls of wealthy dead people:

> For the parish priest and the pardoner divide the silver
> That the poor of the parish should have, but don't get.
> Parsons and parish priests plead to the bishop
> That their parishes are poor, since the pestilence time,
> And they beg for leave to go live in London
> And sing there for simony, for silver is sweet.

(trans. SW)

To many onlookers, the Roman Church of the fourteenth century was too wrapped up in the consequences of its own wealth and power to be able to shed much holy light into the lives of the faithful 'commons' (the contemporary term for the majority of the people, who were neither clerics nor aristocrats). John Wycliffe was among the church's most effective critics: his assertions were all the more devastating because he spoke from a position that was fairly high up within the elite of the church itself.

Wycliffe started his career as a university scholar of unusual distinction. He was soon counted among the loyal followers of John Of Gaunt, one of the richest and most formidable aristocrats in the country. Gaunt seems to have been particularly good at choosing brilliant protégés - Geoffrey Chaucer also lived much of his life within Gaunt's sphere of influence, and even became related to Gaunt by marriage.

Although he was a priest, Wycliffe was useful to the secular part of the English establishment because he was prepared to argue against the power of the Pope. At that time, England was obliged to pay large taxes to the Roman Church, which, like most very rich institutions, always seemed to need more riches. The Pope's power was widely feared and resented: at any time he could stretch out his crook and excommunicate anyone who threatened or displeased him. When one Pope made wars against Florence, he sent out an order to the effect that any Christian was entitled to seize the houses and all the goods of any Florentines he happened to know of. A Pope could also issue a dreadful summons to his Court, to anyone he particularly wanted to speak to. He would sometimes appoint his own men to positions in the priestly hierarchies of Catholic countries, against the wishes of the officials on the ground.

The reputation of the Papacy was greatly diminished during the scandal of the Great Schism (1378 to 1417) when there were two opposing Popes, one in Rome and another at Avignon, and believers had to choose which one they thought was genuine. The situation was further confused by the election of a third pope, Alexander V, in 1409.

Meeting Nicholas III, one of the more notorious Popes, in Hell, the Italian poet Dante upbraids him in startlingly direct language:

> Your avarice
> O'ercasts the world with mourning, under foot
> Treading the good, and raising bad men up.
> (trans. Carey)

Dante's outburst, in Canto XIX of his *Inferno*, is all the more surprising given that his usual response to the tormented souls is fear and pity. Dante also claims to be holding himself back out of respect for the Papal office itself. Nicholas, with many other Simoniacs (people who have made fortunes by abusing their sacred offices) is spending eternity head-down in a hole, the soles of his feet endlessly on fire. It is clear from the facial expression of the Latin poet Virgil, Dante's guide through Hell, that he approves of Dante's bitter speech. Like Langland's *Piers Plowman*, Dante's *Divine Comedy* is a dream-poem, and it is very telling that two authors from different ends of Europe, writing in the same century, should have been so interested in dreams, and also so preoccupied with the corruption of the church.

Having argued in favour of the rights of the English monarch to have more control over matters clerical, Wycliffe went on to set out his increasingly radical ideas about how the church as a whole should be reformed. Such opinions were regarded as heretical and dangerous by both church and state. Various attempts were made to silence Wycliffe, but his princely protectors kept him unharmed during his life. After his death his bones were dug up, burned and scattered in a ceremony that must have seemed terrifying in an age where the resurrection of the body was a widely held doctrine. During his life, the main penalty suffered by Wycliffe for his supposed heresy was to be banished to his rectory of Lutterworth in Leicestershire; a semi-retirement that probably gave him even more time to set out his shocking views.

Wycliffe was keen to expose the abuses of the church of his own day. He was pretty familiar with these abuses because he himself had benefited from them. The Leicestershire rectory to which he was banished was technically his own: it had been a useful source of income to him for years, but he had been an absentee minister. This is precisely the sort of thing he sought to cast shade on in his writing and preaching.

Wycliffe inveigled against churchmen who became too involved with politics, yet he had himself been a tame scholar, working for the political ends of powerful secular men. His doubts about the central role of the priesthood in Christianity are undermined, from our modern perspective, by the fact of his long career as a priest.

What, then, were these ideas that caused Wycliffe to be untimely ripped from his long home? Well, he believed that a priest cannot have any real control over the state or fate of a believer's soul - he felt that God alone could decide if a sinner was really absolved after confession, for instance. He was also doubtful about what was supposed to happen to the bread and wine during communion - his 'realist' approach would not allow him to accept that the priest in charge worked any divine magic on the bread, turning it into the actual flesh of Christ.

From the Quaker perspective, Wycliffe's doubts about the nature of the Lord's Supper may seem trivial, but in the Medieval context it would be hard to exaggerate the radical nature of Wycliffe's views on this central rite. Many historians take their attitude to the Eucharist as the defining idea of the Wycliffites, the followers of Wycliffe, who also became known as the Lollards. If the mysterious nature of the Lord's Supper could be called into question, then the significance of the church and her priests could also be massively diminished. Belief in the centrality and importance of the Eucharist had grown out of all proportion during the fourteen hundred years of Christianity up to Wycliffe's time.

Wycliffe is said to have worked at his writings until the moment of his death, even though he had long been physically hampered by the effects of a stroke. The church tried hard to destroy everything he had written, but by various means some one hundred and thirty-two pieces attributed to him have survived. Some were preserved because they were cherished by the heretical Hussites in Prague, a sect who were heavily influenced by this curmudgeonly English scholar.

Opinions differ as to Wycliffe's relationship to the Lollards, or Wycliffites, who continued to follow his ideas after his death. Whereas MacFarlane (in his *John Wycliffe and the beginnings of English Nonconformity*) tends to downplay Wycliffe's role as the deliberate founder of the group, others picture Wycliffe's rectory of Lutterworth as a sort of training-camp where Lollards received direct instruction from the master. There is a handsome print showing him at the door of his rectory, giving some last words of encouragement to a group of Lollards who are just about to set off. In this print, Wycliffe looks like a particularly venerable headmaster, seeing off a bunch of pupils who are about to go on an outward-bound trip.

Whether or not Wycliffe himself ever gave the group his blessing, the Lollards (the word is from a Dutch word meaning 'mumblers') continued to have a lot of influence until the failure of Sir John Oldcastle's rebellion in 1414.

Oldcastle, said to be one of the originals for Shakespeare's Sir John Falstaff, had been a boon companion of King Henry V until his Lollard beliefs and his political ambitions led to his attempted rebellion in 1414, and his arrest and downfall in 1417. After the disaster of 1414, Lollardy went underground, typically surviving among people of rather humbler origins than the aristocratic Sir John.

In his classic study of the survival of Lollard ideas in Yorkshire into the 16th century, A.G. Dickens tracks specific Lollard doctrines through accusations of heresy preserved in legal documents. G.H.W. Parker, by contrast, shows how the threat of the Lollards helped define the character of conservative mainstream English Christianity in the centuries after its suppression *(The Morning Star: Wycliffe and the dawn of the Reformation, 1965)*. Parker also shows how, partly because of the corruption of the church and its religious houses, Lollard ideas were put into action in the *sixteenth* century (though not under the Lollard name) to aid the reform of the English Church and to further the diminution of the Pope's power over England.

Many of Wycliffe's more extreme views are very much in line with the beliefs of George Fox and the early Quakers. Both sets of ideas tend to diminish the importance of anything resembling a clergy or the Papacy. Many Lollard preachers were not officially ordained priests, and likewise most of the early Quakers were drawn from among lay people. The Lollards had called into question the nature, power and efficacy of the Eucharist – the Quakers went further and rejected all attempts to re-enact the Lord's Supper. Both Lollards and Quakers wholeheartedly embraced the Bible in English, but the Lollards of medieval times could not take the existence or the regular reading of such a book for granted. Books were much rarer in fourteenth century England than they were in the seventeenth century, and illiteracy was more widespread. Scriptures, services and hymns in English were among the cornerstones of the English Reformation: in Wycliffe's England, Latin still dominated religious life, and the Latin Vulgate Bible was central to worship and scholarship. One hundred and fifty-two years after the death of John Wycliffe, the Bible translator William Tyndale was executed, partly because of his presumption in setting the Gospel before the English in their own language.

There are certainly similarities between the ideas of the Lollards and those of the first Quaker George Fox, but, if there was not a surviving Lollard cell in Fox's home village of Fenny Drayton, how else would the first Quaker have found out about a figure of distant history like John Wycliffe?

Foxe's Book of Martyrs

John Wycliffe, the Lollards, William Tyndale and others were presented to the Protestant British as the ancestors of the Reformation in a book - one of the most successful books ever published in England. The book is John Foxe's *Acts and monuments of martyrs*, known as *Foxe's Book of Martyrs*, first published in 1559. From 1571, the book was appearing in churchmen's houses and in the famous chained libraries of English churches. Later, thanks to the miracle of the printing-press, it gained a more widespread and popular readership, passing through many editions.

John Foxe, the author of this extraordinary work, glares out of his engraved portrait printed in the book from a dark, narrow face, lengthened by the addition of an impressive forked beard. Despite his rather forbidding appearance, the grimness of his subject and his status as a tireless champion of Protestantism, Foxe was a compassionate man. He pleaded for the life of the Jesuit Edmund Campion (1540-1581), and for the lives of some hapless Anabaptists discovered in London in 1575, during the reign of Elizabeth I:

For such is my disposition...that I can scarce pass the shambles where beasts are slaughtered, but that my mind secretly recoils with a feeling of pain.

Foxe had been an ardent Roman Catholic when he was a student at Oxford, but was later brought round to the Protestant way by his extensive reading in the scriptures, and in later Christian writings such as those of the Fathers of the Church. It is interesting to note that the unfortunate Campion, who was hanged, drawn and quartered at Tyburn, had gone in the opposite direction, giving up his role as a Deacon of the Church of England to embrace the new and dangerous calling of undercover Jesuit in Elizabethan England. Both men had attended Oxford colleges.

Although he was a working Minister of the Church of England, and sometimes a teacher, John Foxe still found time to research, write and augment his immensely long martyrology. He worked at great speed, sometimes making use of assistance from other, less conscientious scholars, and there are certainly some mistakes here and there among his pages. It seems, however, that very few of Foxe's contemporary martyrs were actually found to be still alive when the accounts of their martyrdoms were published.

John Foxe's martyrology provoked the Roman Catholics of his day into disputing the facts he had presented, and producing their own books of Catholic martyrs.

Foxe's opus is one of those books that were supremely influential for many years, but that are seldom read today. (Other examples might include the plays of Seneca; *The Consolations of philosophy* by Boethius, the works of the Latin poet Lucan and of the English poet Sir Philip Sidney.) The popularity of Foxe's book didn't peter out until quite late in the 19th century, when its sensational narratives and striking engravings still made it attractive Sunday reading, especially in those houses where 'improving books' were supposed to be read on the Christian Sabbath. Some nineteenth century editions of Foxe's book even added accounts of the sufferings of the early Quakers, of the Baptist John Bunyan (author of *The Pilgrim's Progress*) and of John Wesley, the founder of the Methodists.

Foxe's book has fallen out of favour in modern times, perhaps because of its old-fashioned sectarian and patriotic bias, and the general decline of interest in religious reading. Its graphic treatment of the physical realities of martyrdom might have caused some squeamish Victorians to put their old family copies away in the attic. Although the old martyrologies are seldom read today, the idea of martyrdom runs deep in the human spirit, and martyrdom and sainthood are still very much with us in modern times. Since John XXIII became Pope in 1958, some 1,100 saints and martyrs have been added to the official Roman Catholic list. David Barrett and Todd M. Johnson, in their book *Our world and how to reach it*, estimate that well over 26 million Christians were martyred during the twentieth century alone: this makes an average of about 290,000 a year. Barrett and Johnson have come up with a handy definition of martyrs (a word that originally referred to the early Christian 'witnesses' who had actually known Jesus). To Barrett and Johnson, martyrs are 'believers in Christ who lose their lives prematurely, in situations of witness, as a result of human hostility'. Barrett and Johnson's astounding statistics are quoted in Susan Bergman's book on twentieth century martyrs: she also mentions a five-hour ceremony that took place in New York in November of 1981, when 30,000 Russians killed by the Bolsheviks in 1918 were 'canonized and glorified as martyrs'.

In its earlier incarnations, *Foxe's book of martyrs* comprised nothing less than a history of Christianity, but with a heavy emphasis on martyrdoms. Foxe does not concentrate exclusively on martyrs, however: he puts forward for hero-worship many pioneers of religious reform, or of Protestantism *per se* who died with their boots off; including John Wycliffe, Martin Luther and John Calvin. It would be very surprising to learn that George Fox had never had any contact with John Foxe's famous book, given its popularity among the English in his day.

The main political impact of the *Book of martyrs* lay in Foxe's accounts of those Protestants who were martyred under the Roman Catholic Queen Mary (John Foxe himself was eking out a meagre living in exile on the continent during Mary's reign).

The schoolboy chosen to meet Queen Mary with a Latin salutatory when she first entered London as queen later became the Catholic martyr, Edmund Campion, whose fate had aroused John Foxe's compassion. Called 'Bloody Mary' by generations of English Protestants, Mary is one of those fascinating dead-ends of English history. She tried to re-establish Roman Catholicism as the state religion of England. She married the King of Spain, hoping to forge an alliance with the Catholic super-power of the time, but the marriage didn't 'take', as they say, and it proved childless.

During her short reign (1553-1558) Mary's agents attempted to root out Protestantism in England, and brought about the executions of many non-Catholics who dared to put their metaphorical heads above the parapet. These martyrdoms didn't happen very long before George Fox's time: Fox's generation would have been able to look back on them in much the same way as people currently in middle age (at the beginning of the twenty-first century) might look back on the late Victorian period.

The spirit of militant Protestantism in John Foxe's book did not sit well with attempts to move away from the Puritan approach during the difficult reign of King Charles I. During George Fox's lifetime, John Foxe's book was paid the considerable compliment of an official ban. In 1632, the unpopular William Laud, later Archbishop of Canterbury but then Archbishop of London, insisted that only books that had met with his approval should be printed. It seems that the *Book of martyrs* did not meet with the approval of Laud or of his team of censors. The whole system was reminiscent of the Roman Catholic *imprimatur* (whereby books judged to be consistent with Catholic ideas still bear a sort of stamp of approval) and it seems to have had little lasting effect. With the fall of the monarchy, the re-printing of this popular favourite could no longer be suppressed. During the reign of Charles II, however, the attempt to place the presses under the control of the clergy was revived.

In Court at Lancaster

George Fox mentions martyrs and martyrdoms several times in his *Journal*: several of these references reveal a familiarity with the contents of John Foxe's book, or of something very like it. He only mentions a 'Book of Martyrs' by name once, during one of his appearances at Lancaster, in the August of 1664.

The circumstances of the first Quaker's court appearances at this time are to do with some heavy-handed attempts by the Restoration government to suppress minority sects such as the Quakers.

Fox had been engaged to appear at Lancaster to answer charges brought against him under an Act passed in 1662, designed to prevent Quaker Meetings, and to discourage the Quaker practice of refusing to take oaths. This Act was part of a series of laws that came to be known, collectively, as the Clarendon Code, after Chancellor Edward Hyde, 1st Earl of Clarendon, Charles II's chief minister. The Code was introduced by the young and aristocratic Cavalier Parliament (1661-1679) which sought to increase the power and importance of the Anglican Church while simultaneously pushing the various minority sects out to the fringes of the political scene. At this time, Fox and many of his followers were ordered to take an oath of allegiance to the King. Many refused to take the oath, and Fox even declared that he had never taken an oath in his life.

Fox could very easily have evaded his time in prison and in court at Lancaster. He had been ordered to appear, but he had not been locked up 'on remand' as we would say today, until the date of his first court appearance.

Before Judge Turner and Judge Twisden at Lancaster, Fox repeatedly pointed out that the taking of oaths was forbidden in the New Testament. The parts of the New Testament books of Matthew and James that Fox relied on in his condemnation of oaths (Matthew 5:34 and James 5:12) make it clear that the kind of oath that is particularly excluded is an oath invoking something else, outside of the swearer, such as an oath sworn 'by Heaven' or 'by Jerusalem'. In the Matthew passage, Jesus forbids such oaths because they are sworn by things over which the swearer has no power: 'Neither shalt thou swear by thy head, because thou canst not make one hair white or black' (Matt.5, 36). Instead, Jesus wants his followers to say yes or no with complete truthfulness, and not rely on external things as supposed guarantors of a promise.

It is hardly surprising that Fox and the early Quakers should have made so much of this idea: a simple promise made on one's own behalf is a more inward and personal thing than an oath 'by Heaven', and Fox and his followers wanted a religion of inward, and not of outward things.

The Quaker stance against oaths was, nevertheless, something that put them in direct conflict with seventeenth-century English practice. Clearly Exasperated by George Fox's arguments from scripture, Judge Turner came up with his most convincing argument in favour of swearing; arguing, in effect, that it was part of the glue that held society together:

...the King is sworn, the Parliament is sworn, I am sworn, the justices are sworn, and the law is preserved by oaths.

In response to this practical argument, invoking both tradition and present practice, George Fox mentally put the Bible to one side and invoked the 'Book of Martyrs', reminding the court how:

...in the 'Book of Martyrs' how many of the martyrs had refused to swear, both within the time of the ten persecutions [under the Roman Emperors] and in Bishop Bonner's days... [during the reign of Mary]

Earlier, before Judge Twisden, Fox had used a similar argument, but without mentioning the 'Book of Martyrs' by name:

I asked him if he did not know that Christians in the primitive times, under the ten persecutions, and some also of the martyrs in Queen Mary's days, refused swearing, because Christ and the apostle had forbidden it.

There are several examples of oaths being used to trap martyrs in *Foxe's Book of Martyrs*, any of which might have been in George Fox's mind that day at Lancaster. Perhaps the most terrifying instance of refusal of an oath leading to martyrdom happened under the Emperor Maximian in AD 286. John Foxe recounts how a Roman legion, consisting entirely of Christians, refused a Pagan oath of allegiance to their emperor. The legion was decimated twice (that is, one in ten of the soldiers were killed) but still the survivors stood firm. At last, the entire legion was slaughtered.

Fox's sense of Christian history, as passed down to him via the Bible and the *Book of martyrs*, was evidently a source of great strength to him. He clearly saw his own mission as a continuation of this simultaneously glorious and bitter tradition. The connection Fox indicates, between the Primitive Christian martyrs, the Marian martyrs, and Friends, is further proof that, in William Penn's phrase, Quakerism was supposed to be 'Primitive Christianity Revived'.

John Foxe, the author of the *Book of Martyrs*, died too early to have known anything about the Quakers, but the grim inheritance of broadly Protestant and Lollard martyrs, from those ancient martyrs of the Early Church, was part of the message of his book. This message was clearly not lost on the first Quaker.

In prison at Lancaster, George Fox had been busy writing. That he was preoccupied by thoughts of the Early Church at this time is borne out by his assertion that he had 'answered' (i.e. discredited) the claims of the Roman Catholic, Anglican, Presbyterian and Independent churches in his writings. He asserts that these 'are the four chief religions that are got up since the apostles' days'. Clearly, Fox felt that he was an adherent of the true old religion, of Primitive Christianity, and that the churches that had appeared since apostolic times were mere upstarts.

Joyce Lewes of Mancetter

As well as his sense of himself as an inheritor of the tradition of the martyrs, George Fox seems to have had a family connection with the contents of John Foxe's book as well: right at the start of his *Journal* he mentions that his mother's maiden name was Lago, and that she was 'of the stock of the martyrs'. Rufus Jones believed that she was connected in some way to the Mancetter Martyrs, whose sufferings are related in some detail in Foxe's martyrology.

Mancetter is very near to George Fox's home village of Fenny Drayton in Leicestershire, and the story of the local Marian martyrs was probably well-known in the area in Fox's time. John Foxe relates the sufferings of poor Joyce Lewes of Mancetter in a way that is at the same time sectarian, patriotic, proud and angry.

Joyce, wife of Thomas Lewes of Mancetter, was strangely distressed to hear of the martyrdom of one Laurence Saunders at Coventry. Saunders had been a critic of the new Catholic state as established under Queen Mary. He had also been a supporter of the Protestant reforms of Henry VIII's short-lived son and heir, King Edward VI.

Joyce Lewes, who seems to have been a vain and frivolous woman for most of her life, at some point came under the influence of her neighbour John Glover, who had corresponded with the unfortunate Saunders. Glover, who later died of an 'ague' resulting from his attempts to hide in a forest and thus escape the authorities, persuaded Joyce that the Roman Catholic Mass was an evil thing. Her husband still forced Joyce to attend Masses, however.

When the congregation was sprinkled with the holy water, Joyce turned her back, thus showing her objection to the new Catholic *status quo*. When a summoner was sent to her house to summon her (of course) to an interrogation, her husband made this official eat the summons, quite literally. This initial reception notwithstanding, Joyce Lewes was eventually taken, interrogated, imprisoned, found guilty and condemned to be burned at the stake.

With the help of her consoling friends, she bore her imprisonment pretty well, even though 'Sathan' tempted her to despair. She drank a toast to the downfall of the 'idolatrous masse' just before she was executed, and a lot of the onlookers at the burning seem to have agreed with her anti-Catholic opinions. Attempts by an 'old priest' to take note of the identities of her supporters did not lead to any arrests; something which John Foxe apparently regarded as an example of divine providence.

The story of Joyce Lewes has many features that make it like a story of one of the later, Quaker, saints. To begin with, it is the story of an independent-minded woman whose actions are not ruled by her husband. This is reminiscent of Margaret Fell, who harboured George Fox without first asking for the permission of her powerful husband, Judge Fell. Joyce Lewes is looked after by sympathetic friends, much as later Quaker prisoners were helped by Friends from local Meetings. Although she is described as a gentlewoman, Joyce Lewes lived in an obscure provincial village, very like those from which many of the first Quakers came. Joyce's conversion to a new view of religion goes hand-in-hand with the general reformation of her manners - this is like the sudden sobriety that came upon that famous Quaker of a later age, Elizabeth Fry.

In Joyce Lewes's case her religious conversion (Fox would call it 'convincement') happened not in any official place of worship, but in her own or a neighbour's house, and was inspired by a man who was not an ordained priest. These factors are also reminiscent of later, Quaker, convincements.

Other Leicestershire martyrs of this period included Thomas Moore, a domestic servant, killed under Queen Mary in 1556, and the famous Hugh Latimer, known as one of the Oxford martyrs, born at Thurcaston in Leicestershire, who was burned at the stake at Oxford in the October of 1555.

Anthony Nutter

An example of religious persecution too late to be included in Foxe's book took place in George Fox's home village of Fenny Drayton only nineteen years before Fox's birth. In his Quaker history, *A portrait in grey*, John Punshon points out that Fox's father, Christopher 'Righteous Christer' Fox was probably officially involved with the Fenny Drayton Parish Church where it happened, and at the time it took place.

The whole story of the deprivation of the Puritan minister Anthony Nutter can be said to have started in 1572, during the reign of Elizabeth I, when the Puritans issued their *Admonition to Parliament.*

The *Admonition*, supposed to have been written by John Field and Thomas Wilcox, advocated wholesale reforms of the English Church, many of them designed to bring the church more in line with what were thought to be the practices of Primitive Christianity. The Puritans wanted to:

Take away the Lordship, the loytering, the pompe, the idlenes, and livings of Bishops, but yet employ them to such ends as they were in the old churche apointed for. Let a lawful and a godly Seignorie look that they preache, not quarterly or monthly, but continually: not for filthy lucre's sake but of a ready mynde.

They contrasted what they supposed happened in the Early Church with what happened in their own times when the Eucharist was administered:

They ministered the Sacrament plainely. We pompously with singing, pypying, surplesse and cope wearyng.

Also in 1572, a group of Puritans established the first English *presbytery* at Wandsworth. This was an experiment in a more 'levelling' form of church government, and was received as an implied criticism of the hierarchical episcopal system (characterised by the existence of bishops) which still persists in the Anglican Church today.

According to A.L. Rowse, groups of presbyteries soon formed into 'classis', alliances which made it possible for the Puritan clergy to have their own meetings where, it seems, extempore prayers were a feature.

John Punshon tells us that the Puritan Anthony Nutter became rector of Fenny Drayton in 1582, and in 1590 was imprisoned as one of the leaders of the English Presbyterian Movement. His deprivation came during the reign of James I.

James was King of Scotland before he was invited to become King of England as well. Before he even got to London for the first time, he was presented with the *Millenary Petition*, supposedly agreed to by 'more than a thousand' clergymen, in 1603. Like the earlier *Admonition*, delivered to one of his predessessor's parliaments, the *Petition* humbly begged for the reshaping of the English Church along more Puritan lines. The authors urged, among other things, that:

...the longsomeness of service[s be] abridged, Church songs and music moderated to better edification; that the Lord's Day be not profaned; the rest upon holy days not so strictly urged; that there may be a uniformity of doctrine prescribed; no popish opinion to be any more taught or defended...

In response to the *Admonition*, the new king arranged a meeting of churchmen to discuss religious reform at Hampton Court in 1604. King James fancied himself as an intellectual, and perhaps he relished the chance to debate religious matters at his redbrick palace.

Some accounts of this frank exchange of views make it sound like an unruly game of theological volleyball, with the bishops on one side of the net and the Puritans on the other. It had been going quite nicely until one of the Puritans let slip the fatal word 'presbytery'. This caused James to fly into a rage, supposing that something like Scottish Presbyterianism was intended by the English Puritans. When he was 'only' King of Scotland, James had tried to limit the growing influence of Presbyterianism, not least by imprisoning Andrew Melville (1545-1622), its chief advocate in his kingdom at that time. Melville's proposals seemed designed to take any power over the church out of the hands of the monarch, who tried to balance Melville's ideas against a more traditional, hierarchical system based on the power of the bishops.

The King was obviously not prepared to have to deal with Presbyterianism in his new kingdom as well. That day at Hampton, James cried that, 'It [Presbyterianism] agreeth as well with monarchy, as God with the Devil,' and added that 'I will harry them [the Presbyterians] out of the land, or else do worse.'

The consequences were considerable. James later insisted that all the English clergy would have to subscribe to the existing form of the church by December 1604. Some three hundred clergy refused, and were deprived of their livings. One of these was Anthony Nutter of Fenny Drayton.

As he grew up, George Fox must surely have been aware of how the hand of the monarch had reached inside the little parish church in his village, and extracted a rector who probably had the support of many of the villagers and of the Purefoys, their Puritan landlords. This had happened under the king who died in the year of Fox's birth. As Trevelyan points out, (in *England under the Stuarts*, Methuen, 1965) the hundreds of clergy deprived in 1604-5

37

suddenly became sectaries: this was a schism, and such schisms had not often happened in the English Church before.

Foxe's Book of martyrs, and oral traditions about more recently persecutions, were probably part of the religious education George Fox received at the hands of his mother Mary Fox, nee Lago.

Lichfield

A very striking example of Fox's connection with the idea of martyrdom occurred in 1651, when the first Quaker visited Lichfield. In a radical departure from his usual approach, Fox entered the cathedral city barefoot, and walked about the streets raving about 'the bloody city of Lichfield'. He seems to have been mystified by his own behaviour on this occasion, until he learned about a mass martyrdom supposed to have happened in the city in Roman times. In Lichfield, Fox believed himself to have had some sort of mystical connection with an historic martyrdom.

Rufus Jones thought that Fox's behaviour at Lichfield might also have been connected to the fate of Edward Wightman, burned at the stake at Lichfield in April 1612. Wightman was the last person to be executed in this way by the authorities in England. He was a minister of the Six-Principle Baptist Church, and his crimes seem to have included his belief that he personally was some sort of prophet or messiah. Whereas George Fox might have agreed with some of Wightman's ideas, such as his rejection of the trinity, of creeds and of infant baptism, he would certainly not have been impressed by his delusions of grandeur. Whether Fox knew that Wightman's father came from Burbage, just a few miles down Watling Street from Fenny Drayton, is not known. It is certainly the case that Fox's uncle, Pickering, was also a Baptist, and that Fox sought him out when he was in London.

CONCLUSION

It is customary for students of the history of anything, not just religion, to find connections between ideas that arose at one point in history, and similar ideas that appeared at an earlier period. The evidence for such connections – often called 'influences', may be extremely explicit: an example of an explicit connection of this sort would be George Fox's reference to the *Book of Martyrs*, before Judge Turner in 1664. Such connections or influences can also be very vague and general and hard to pin down.

It is pretty obvious that George Fox was influenced by the Bible and *The book of martyrs*: he mentions these influences by name. Through *Foxe's book of martyrs*, which is probably what he means by 'The book of Martyrs', George Fox would have been brought into contact with the lives, ideas and personalities of many heroes of Christianity. Because of the bias of John Foxe's book, the youthful *George* Fox might have been particularly impressed by tales of the heroes of Protestantism and of other movements for religious reform.

The Bible and John Foxe are explicit influences for George Fox. Despite various attempts to do so, it is more difficult to trace any definite influence from continental mystics such as Eckhart, Boehme and their followers with any certainty, because George Fox himself does not mention them by name. The researcher in this area is tempted to point to striking 'parallels' and to invoke the 'zeitgeist' or the ideas known to be 'in the air' in George Fox's England, but little in the way of a decisive link can be found.

The degree to which the nature and content of George Fox's mystical experiences were dictated by any received traditions is hard to judge: as Rufus Jones and William James knew, profound mystical experiences undergone by people from very different times and places bear an uncanny resemblance to each other. The attempt to trace George Fox's influences is further frustrated by three factors – Fox's known lack of much in the way of formal education, his tendency to internalize ideas and to make them part of his own system of thought, and the tendency for certain Christian ideas to reappear, as if spontaneously, under different names at different times throughout

Christian history. These recurring ideas obsessed such men as John Wycliffe, William Tyndale and Martin Luther, and they seem to be rediscovered or even re-invented by every new generation of believers, even among Christians who have no knowledge of their previous incarnations.

Some of the more radical ideas that George Fox rediscovered, or perhaps reinvented, as part of his mission, are to do with the necessity or otherwise of a trained, elite priesthood, and the possibility that direct mystical experience of God could still influence Christian belief in what to Fox would have been modern times.

It was part of George Fox's mission to expose these ideas to a fierce and searching light. Modern-day Quakers all over the world are still addressing them in their thoughts, their utterances and their lives. George Fox was quite aware that he was not the first to consider these things: indeed he drew strength from the fact that others had addressed them before him. He was not overly concerned with identifying all the sources of his thoughts to his readers or listeners. He is a good example of an original thinker who achieves originality by transforming tradition. His answers to the recurring Christian questions were so radical that he and his followers were regarded as dangerous revolutionaries, deserving harassment, prison and even execution.

SELECT BIBLIOGRAPHY

Ashley, Maurice: *England in the seventeenth century (1603-1714)*. Penguin, 1958

Backhouse, Halcyon (ed.): *The cloud of unknowing*, Hodder & Stoughton, 1985

Backhouse, Halcyon (ed.): *Meister Eckhart*, Hodder & Stoughton, 1992

Bergman, Susan (ed.): *A cloud of witnesses: 20th century martyrs*, Fount, 1996

Bittle, William G.: *James Nayler 1618-1660: the Quaker indicted by parliament*, Sessions, 1986

Blamires, David: *Eckhart, Rufus Jones and the Quaker tradition* in *The Friends Quarterly*, July 2006

Boehme, Jacob: *The way to Christ*, translated by Peter Erb, Paulist Press, 1978

Braithwaite, William C: *The beginnings of Quakerism*, Sessions, 1970

Brewer, Derek: *Chaucer in his time*, Longman, 1973

Butler, Samuel: *Hudibras*, Oxford, 1967

Carlton, Charles: *Archbishop William Laud*, Routledge, 1987

Chadwick, Henry: *Augustine*, Oxford, 1986

Chaucer, Geoffrey: *The Canterbury tales*, Oxford, 1906

Chaucer, Geoffrey: *The Romaunt of the Rose* in *The complete works of Geoffrey Chaucer*, edited by F.N. Robinson, Oxford, 1974

Chenu, Bruno, et al: *The book of Christian martyrs*, SCM, 1990

Chesterton, G.K.: *Stories, essays & poems*, Dent, 1935

Coote, Stephen: *Royal survivor: a life of Charles II*, Hodder & Stoughton, 1999

Dante: *The vision of Dante Alighieri or Hell, Purgatory and Paradise*: translated by H.F. Cary, Dent, 1908

Dickens, A.G.: *Lollards and Protestants in the Diocese of York, 1509-1558*, University of Hull, 1959

Dupre, Louis: *The deeper life*, Crossroads, 1981

Fox, George: *Journal of George Fox*, Dent, 1962

Fox, George: *The Journal of George Fox*, revised edition, edited by John L. Nickalls, Society of Friends, 1975

Fox, George: *Journal of George Fox*, FUP, 1983

Foxe, John: *Foxe's book of martyrs: updated and abridged*, Barber, 2001

Grainger, Roger: *Watching for wings: theology and mental illness in a pastoral setting*, Darton, Longman and Todd, 1979

Grant, Patrick: *A dazzling darkness*, Fount, 1985

Hildegard of Bingen: *Hildegard of Bingen; an anthology*, edited by Fiona Bowie and Oliver Davies, SPCK, 1992

Hill, Christopher: *The world turned upside-down*, Penguin, 1975

Hudson, Anne (ed.): *Selections from English Wycliffite writings*, University of Toronto, 1997

Huxley, Aldous: *The doors of perception*, Flamingo, 1994

James, William: *The varieties of religious experience*, Longmans, 1913

Jones, Mary Hoxie: *Rufus M. Jones*, FHS, 1970

Jones, Rufus M.: *The faith & practice of the Quakers*, Methuen, 1938

Langland, William: *Piers the plowman*, Oxford, 1923

Langland, William: *Piers the ploughman*, translated by G.F. Goodridge, Penguin, 1966

Lewis, I.M.: *Ecstatic religion*, Penguin, 1971

Lynch, Michael: *The Interregnum 1649-60*, Hodder & Stoughton, 1994

Mackay, Charles: *Extraordinary popular delusions and the madness of crowds*, Wordsworth, 1995

McFarlane, KB: *John Wycliffe and the beginnings of English Nonconformity*, English Universities Press, 1952

Moorman, J.R.H.: *A history of the Church in England*, 3rd edition, A&C Black, 1973

Millward, J.S. (ed.): *Portraits and documents: seventeenth century*, Hutchinson, 1961

Parker, G.H.W.: *The Morning Star: Wycliffe and the dawn of the Reformation*, Paternoster, 1965

Penn, William: *The peace of Europe, the fruits of solitude and other writings*, Dent, 1993

Punshon, John: *A portrait in grey*, QHS, 1984

Rowse, A.L.: *The England of Elizabeth*, Reprint Society, 1953

Rupp, Gordon: *Six makers of English religion 1500-1700*, Hodder, 1964

Scruton, Roger: *Spinoza*, Oxford, 1986

Taylor, Ernest E.: *The Valiant Sixty*, Bannisdale, 1947

Thrall, Margaret E.: *The Cambridge Bible commentary: I and II Corinthians*, Cambridge, 1965

Trevelyan, G.M.: *England under the Stuarts*, Methuen, 1965

Tuchman, Barbara: *A distant mirror: the calamitous 14th century*, Macmillan, 1979

Underhill, Evelyn: *Mysticism*, Methuen, 1960

Watts, Fraser: *Theology and psychology*, Ashgate, 2002

White, Victor: *God and the unconscious*, Fontana, 1960

Wooley, Benjamin: *The Queen's conjuror: the science and magic of Dr Dee*, Flamingo, 2002

Wright, Tom: *Paul for everyone: 2 Corinthians*, SPCK, 2003

SOME USEFUL WEBSITES:

Bartleby online books:
www.bartleby.com

British History:
www.british-history.ac.uk

Catholic Encyclopaedia Online:
www.newadvent.org/cathen/index.html

Christian Classics Ethereal Library:
www.ccel.org

English Dissenters:
www.exlibris.org/nonconform/engdis/

Foxe's Book of Martyrs:
www.hrionline.ac.uk/foxe

Gutenberg Project – online books:
www.gutenberg.org

Hanover Historical Texts Project:
www.history.hanover.edu/texts

Jacob Boehme:
www.pegasus.cc.ucf.edu/janzb/boehme/home.html

Jane Lead:
www.passtheword.org/Jane-Lead/index.html

Wikipedia:
http://en.Wikipedia.org/wiki